CALVIN *Coolidge*

CALVIN *Coolidge*

OUR THIRTIETH PRESIDENT

By Melissa Maupin

SPIRIT
of America™

The Child's World®, Inc.
Chanhassen, Minnesota

6

CALVIN *Coolidge*

Published in the United States of America by The Child's World®, Inc.
PO Box 326 • Chanhassen, MN 55317-0326 • 800-599-READ • www.childsworld.com

Acknowledgments
   The Creative Spark: Mary Francis-DeMarois, Project Director; Elizabeth Sirimarco Budd, Series Editor;
   Robert Court, Design and Art Direction; Janine Graham, Page Layout; Jennifer Moyers, Production

   The Child's World®, Inc.: Mary Berendes, Publishing Director; Red Line Editorial, Fact Research;
   Cindy Klingel, Curriculum Advisor; Robert Noyed, Historical Advisor

Photos
   Cover: White House Collection, courtesy White House Historical Association; ©Bettmann/Corbis: 18, 21, 22,
   29; Courtesy of the Calvin Coolidge Memorial Room, Forbes Library, Northampton, Massachusetts: 14,
   15; Collections of the Library of Congress: 12, 13, 16, 20, 23, 24, 25, 26, 30, 32, 33, 36; The New York
   Public Library: 27; © Underwood & Underwood/CORBIS: 28; Courtesy of the Vermont Historical
   Society: 6, 7, 8, 9, 11, 35

Registration
   The Child's World®, Inc., Spirit of America™, and their associated logos are the sole property and
   registered trademarks of The Child's World®, Inc.

Library of Congress Cataloging-in-Publication Data
   Maupin, Melissa, 1958–
      Calvin Coolidge : our thirtieth president / Melissa Maupin.
         p. cm.
      Includes bibliographical references and index.

      ISBN 1-56766-864-X (lib. bdg. : alk. paper)
      1. Coolidge, Calvin,—1872–1933—Juvenile literature. 2. Presidents—United States—
   Biography—Juvenile literature. [1. Coolidge, Calvin, 1872–1933. 2. Presidents] I. Title.
      E792 .M38 2001
      973.91'5'092—dc21

                                                      00-011460

12   25   32

Contents

Chapter ONE

Silent Cal

Calvin Coolidge was a shy boy who preferred to listen instead of talk. All his life, he would be known as a quiet man. When he became the 30th president, his nickname was "Silent Cal."

CALVIN COOLIDGE GREW UP IN A QUIET HOME in Plymouth Notch, Vermont. His father was a big, strong man who believed in wasting nothing—including words! Calvin's mother, Victoria, was frail and often sick. Calvin and his younger sister, Abigail, had to be quiet and well behaved so they didn't disturb her. Calvin was also naturally shy. Many years later, when Calvin Coolidge led the United States as its president, he would become famous for his quiet personality.

Calvin Coolidge was born on July 4, 1872, in a cottage in Plymouth Notch. His father, John, farmed on the green rolling countryside of Vermont that Calvin would grow to love. John Coolidge also owned the town's general store. He served as tax collector

and justice of the peace. He also was elected to the Vermont legislature, the part of the government that makes the state's laws.

Calvin's father, John, owned the general store and post office in their hometown.

Calvin was smaller than other children his age. He had clear, blue eyes and red hair that gradually changed to dark blond. Because he was small, he didn't feel comfortable playing sports. He enjoyed horseback riding and fishing, however. He also helped his father on the farm, picking apples and collecting sap to make maple syrup.

Calvin's mother, Victoria, died when he was just 12 years old. For the rest of his life, he always carried a photograph of her.

Calvin enjoyed a peaceful, happy life until his mother suffered a horrible accident. When he was 12 years old, she was thrown from a runaway horse and severely injured. Already weak, Victoria Coolidge died soon after the accident. Years later, Calvin Coolidge looked back sadly on her death, saying, "The greatest grief that can come to a boy came to me. Life was never the same again." Calvin attended high school at the Black River Academy in the town of Ludlow, 12 miles away. He lived at the academy and sometimes walked home on weekends to visit his family. In the summers, he would come home and help his father run the farm. Calvin was a good student, known for his wit and his dry sense of humor.

During his senior year, Calvin Coolidge suffered another tragic loss. His sister Abigail became gravely ill. Calvin stayed at Abigail's bedside as she grew weaker and then died. The only way Calvin could deal with his grief was by studying even harder and preparing for college.

Right before Calvin's first year at Amherst College in Massachusetts, John Coolidge remarried. His new wife, Carrie, was a teacher whom Calvin liked and respected.

Calvin struggled during his first two years of college, but his grades improved in the final two years. He graduated with honors in 1895. With only a general goal of what he wanted to do in life, Calvin decided to become a lawyer. After

At Amherst College, Calvin took his studies seriously, although the first two years were difficult for him. Finally, he graduated with honors and decided to study law.

▸ The following poem was one of Coolidge's favorites. He framed it and hung it on his living room wall. How was Coolidge like the owl in the poem?
A wise old owl
lived in an oak.
The more he saw,
the less he spoke.
The less he spoke
the more he heard.
Why can't we be
like that old bird?

▸ As a child, Coolidge was nicknamed "Red" because of his red hair.

▸ Coolidge's name at birth was John Calvin Coolidge. In college, he went by J. Calvin, and as a young adult, he dropped the "John" and went by Calvin.

graduation, he began working as an assistant at a law firm in Northampton, Massachusetts. He also studied for the exams that he would have to pass to become a lawyer. Two years later, he earned his certificate to work as a lawyer and opened his own office.

As he worked to find clients, Coolidge also worked for the Republican Party, one of the country's two major **political parties.** His efforts paid off. Within a year, Coolidge was elected to a seat on the Northampton city council. It was the first of many positions in **politics** that he would hold on his way to the White House. Over the next few years, Coolidge would be elected as city attorney and clerk of courts for Hampshire County.

During this time, he lived in a simple boarding house. Next door to this house was a school for deaf children. A young teacher, Grace Goodhue, worked at the school. One day when she was watering flowers outside, Grace caught a glimpse of Coolidge through his window. He was wearing long underwear and shaving. Grace laughed at the sight, and Coolidge turned to see her leaving. He found out her name and asked to be introduced to her.

Grace was the opposite of Coolidge in many ways. For one thing, she had a warm, friendly personality and rarely felt shy. Still, they liked each other right away and married on October 4, 1905. She was the only woman he had ever dated. A year later, Coolidge was elected to the Massachusetts House of Representatives. He was reelected the next year but resigned after that **term.** By then, he and Grace had two sons, John and Calvin Jr.

Coolidge's next move was to **campaign** to become the mayor of Northampton. Despite his shyness, he made a big effort to meet the voters. Sometimes he stopped people on the street and asked them to vote for him. People found that he was a simple, straightforward man, and he won the election.

After Victoria Coolidge died, Calvin's father married Carrie Brown. They are shown here many years later with their grandson, John.

CALVIN COOLIDGE WAS KNOWN TO BE QUIET AND SHY, BUT HE HAD another side. With people he knew well, he talked easily. Friends even called him talkative. Coolidge was well read and could discuss almost any subject.

Coolidge was not fond of giving speeches, yet he gave more than any other president. At meetings with reporters, called press conferences, Coolidge often gave short answers. Still, he held more of these meetings than any other president. When he met with reporters, he asked them not to take notes, but he let them take his picture. In fact, Coolidge seemed to enjoy posing for the camera. He would even dress up in costumes, such as a Native American headdress. Coolidge was also the first president to star in a film. He let a director film a silent movie about him. Coolidge wore a cowboy costume in one part of the film.

Chapter TWO

The Coolidge Luck

Coolidge served as the mayor of Northampton for two terms.

As CALVIN COOLIDGE'S CAREER BLOSSOMED, many people felt that he was unusually lucky. He certainly seemed to be in the right place at the right time. But he also worked hard for his success. After serving two terms as mayor, Coolidge won a place in the Massachusetts State Senate. He served two terms and planned to leave politics. Right before he announced this, he heard something interesting. The president of the Senate, Levi Greenwood, was leaving to run for the position of lieutenant governor. A lieutenant governor is second in command of a state government and assists the governor. Coolidge decided to run for the Senate again with the hope of receiving the president's seat the following term. But Greenwood changed his mind. Instead of running for lieutenant governor, Greenwood ran for president of the Senate again. As "Coolidge luck" would have it, however, Greenwood lost his seat in the Senate. Coolidge campaigned for the spot as president and was elected.

In 1915, Coolidge ran for lieutenant governor of Massachusetts. This meant that he had to travel across the state to

campaign. At times, his shyness was still a problem. He often felt uncomfortable talking to strangers. "When I was a little fellow, I would go into a panic if I heard strange voices in the kitchen," he once said. "I felt I couldn't meet the people and shake hands with them … the hardest thing in the world was to have to go through the kitchen door and give them a greeting.

Grace Coolidge was a great help to her husband. Her warm personality charmed everyone she met and won support for her husband. A friend once said, "One of Coolidge's greatest assets is Mrs. Coolidge. She will make friends wherever she goes."

I'm all right with old friends, but every time I meet a stranger, I've got to go through the old kitchen door—and it's not easy."

Coolidge won his bid for lieutenant governor and served three terms. He moved to Boston, but Mrs. Coolidge stayed in Northampton and raised the boys. After his third term, Coolidge ran for governor. One of his biggest supporters was Frank Stearns, a wealthy businessman. Stearns backed Coolidge as a **candidate** and continued to support him throughout his career. When the votes were counted, Coolidge won by almost 17,000.

As governor, he fought for better working conditions for the people. He approved a **bill** to limit the workweek to 40 hours for women and children.

He helped pass a law to raise the amount of money workers received from employers if they were injured at work. Coolidge also worked to solve a housing shortage so that **veterans** of World War I could find decent places to live.

The most famous challenge that Coolidge faced as governor was the 1919 Boston police strike. This situation could have hurt Coolidge's career. Instead, the problem turned into another lucky boost for him. Police at that time performed difficult, dangerous work, just as they do today. But in Coolidge's time, they worked long hours for very little pay. In addition, they had to pay for their own uniforms. The police banded together to form a union, a group that fought for better pay and working conditions. The Boston police commissioner said that they could not be in a union and still perform their duties. Seventy-five percent of Boston's police force angrily decided to leave their jobs.

With few police, mobs roamed through the streets, robbing and rioting. Citizens locked themselves in their houses and armed

When policemen went on strike in Boston in 1919, mobs ran wild. Traffic was out of control, and rioters tossed bricks through windows. Calvin Coolidge finally ordered the National Guard to take control of the situation in Scollay Square, shown below.

themselves with guns for protection. The next morning, the mayor of Boston, Andrew Peters, called in the state **militia** to take control of the city. Riots still broke out that night. Two men were killed, and nine were wounded. The next day, Governor Coolidge called in the Massachusetts National Guard. They restored peace to Boston.

The police commissioner fired all the striking policemen. Coolidge supported this decision, even though he believed the policemen deserved higher pay and better working conditions. He explained his support of the commissioner by saying, "There is no right to strike against the public safety by anybody, anywhere, any time!"

Word spread around the country about the strike and Coolidge's bold words. Many people admired how he had handled the situation. Even President Woodrow Wilson sent a note of congratulations to Coolidge. The police strike made him a popular candidate. He easily won reelection as governor.

In 1920, members of the Republican Party held their national convention, where they would choose their next candidate for president of the United States. Frank Stearns supported Coolidge as a candidate, but other convention **delegates** did not. In fact, no candidate won enough votes for a **nomination.** Finally, several powerful senators held a secret meeting. They decided they wanted Ohio Senator Warren G. Harding to be their candidate.

Warren G. Harding (right) ran for president in the 1920 election, with Calvin Coolidge as the vice presidential candidate.

When the delegates met again the next day, the group of senators managed to push through Harding's name as the Republican candidate. Coolidge's luck came into play again. The same group of senators tried to nominate Irvine L. Lenroot as the vice presidential candidate. This upset many delegates who felt that the group wanted too much power. A delegate from Oregon stood up in protest and nominated Coolidge. Soon, others stood and shouted his name: "Coolidge! Coolidge! Coolidge!" In the end, he won a surprising victory and became the Republican vice presidential candidate.

20

PRESIDENT COOLIDGE enjoyed sleeping. Although he started his days early, he also finished them early. Dinner was served at six o'clock, and bedtime came shortly after nine or ten—at the latest. He did not believe in working nights and thought a person who couldn't finish his work in the daytime was not smart. After lunch, Coolidge took a nap each day. Including his nap, he was said to have slept about 11 hours a day. People joked about Coolidge's sleeping habits, and he laughed along with them. One night, he was watching a play when the famous actor, Groucho Marx, saw him in the audience. From the stage, Marx asked, "Isn't it past your bedtime, Calvin?"

Coolidge's vice president, Charles Dawes, was also known for taking regular naps. One time, Dawes's napping got him into trouble. The Senate was deciding whether to approve a man that Coolidge wanted for his **cabinet.** They had reached a tie vote on the issue. Dawes could cast the vote to break the tie in favor of Coolidge's choice. The trouble was, no one could find him. Later they discovered that Dawes had slipped away to take a nap! Coolidge's choice lost the approval of the Senate for the cabinet position.

Chapter THREE

Stepping in as President

Calvin Coolidge was sworn in as vice president in 1921.

COOLIDGE AND HARDING WERE AN ODD-looking pair. Harding was a large, handsome, cheerful man. Coolidge had a slight build and often wore a serious expression. Still, the men liked each other and worked well together. As a team, they had no trouble winning the election. In early 1921, Coolidge became the vice president of the United States.

At his new job as vice president, Coolidge's main duty was to oversee the Senate. He had to keep things running smoothly and stop senators from talking too long. Coolidge rarely interrupted, however. He ran the Senate in his usual calm, silent way. President Harding also allowed him to sit in on cabinet meetings, but Coolidge rarely spoke at them. Another duty he had was to travel across the country to give speeches, explaining President Harding's views. He still wasn't comfortable speaking, however. His speeches and answers to questions were usually brief. Soon Americans were calling him "Silent Cal."

Coolidge was the most uncomfortable at official dinners and social events. At these gatherings, Mrs. Coolidge produced a warm smile and talked easily with people, while Calvin Coolidge said as little as possible. At a dinner party one evening, the woman sitting next to him said, "You must talk to me, Mr. Coolidge. I made a bet today that I could get more than two words out of you." Using his famous dry wit, Coolidge turned to the woman and said, "You lose." That is all he said to her for the rest of the dinner.

Harding and Coolidge made a good team. They liked each other and worked well together. Neither man had any way of knowing that before Harding could finish his term, Coolidge would rise to the presidency.

Some people thought that Grace and Calvin Coolidge were an unlikely couple. Grace was warm, friendly, and talkative. She loved dancing, ice-skating, and going to the theater. Calvin was quiet and sometimes glum. He wasn't interested in music or plays. Nonetheless, they had a happy and strong marriage. "From our beginning together," said Calvin, "we seemed naturally to come to care for each other."

In 1923, President Harding took a long trip across the country, into Canada, and all the way to Alaska. On August 2, he was resting in a hotel in San Francisco while his wife read to him. Suddenly, he shuddered and collapsed. Within a short time, he died. The cause of Harding's death was probably a heart attack.

Coolidge and his family were visiting his father in Vermont at the time of the president's tragic death. Coolidge and Grace had gone to bed early. At 10:45, the nearest Western Union station received a telegram reporting the news about Harding. A messenger and several reporters arrived at John Coolidge's house hours later to deliver the news. John woke his son. Calvin Coolidge dressed and then realized that the United States had no president. He asked his father, who was a **notary public,** to swear him into office. The humble ceremony took place in John Coolidge's sitting room by the light of a kerosene lamp.

President Coolidge was different from President Harding. Harding had allowed gambling, drinking, and late-night parties in the White House. Coolidge wanted no part of those activities. He wanted to restore dignity to the White House. Despite his serious personality, Coolidge did have a light side. He liked exploring all the rooms of the White House. He especially enjoyed ringing the bells and buzzers in his office just to see the staff run to his side. For relaxation, Coolidge went window-shopping, sometimes taking his sons with him. On weekends, he was fond of cruising with Mrs. Coolidge on the presidential yacht, the *Mayflower.*

Coolidge kept all of Harding's cabinet members—but not for very long. Shortly after

News of President Harding's death reached Coolidge while he was visiting family in Vermont. His father administered the oath of office to Coolidge.

Coolidge and Harding (second and third from right, first row) posed for a formal photograph with Harding's cabinet. No one knows for sure how much Harding knew about the Teapot Dome Scandal, but many Americans were upset when they learned about it. The once-popular President Harding became known for the misdeeds of his cabinet. Fortunately for President Coolidge, the American people believed he was not involved.

Coolidge was sworn in as president, a **scandal** surfaced. The government owned land in Wyoming called the Teapot Dome. There was oil on the land, and oil companies wanted to lease it. They offered cabinet member Albert B. Fall $300,000 to lease them the land. Two other members of Harding's cabinet helped Fall make the deal and then cover it up.

Word leaked out about the **bribe,** and the Senate investigated it. Coolidge was a very honest man. The scandal made him angry. "Let the guilty be punished," he said. Albert Fall was convicted of bribery and made to pay $100,000. He also had to spend a year in prison. The other two men resigned in shame. The men were from the president's own political party and were members of his cabinet. The scandal could have been a bad mark on Coolidge's presidency. Instead, the event strengthened his leadership. The American people believed he handled the problem well. They believed he was an honest man.

THE KU KLUX KLAN WAS A HATE GROUP that started in the southern United States after the Civil War. The members did not accept people who were not white or who belonged to certain religions. The Klan hated blacks, Catholics, and Jews. Klansmen wore long robes and masks with pointed hats so that no one would recognize them.

Klan members burned crosses to scare people they did not like. They kidnapped some people and beat and killed others. In some cities, the police failed to arrest or jail Klansmen. In the 1920s, the Klan grew quickly. In 1924, as many as five million people belonged to the Ku Klux Klan. Some members held political offices or were successful businesspeople. During the presidential campaign of 1924, the problems with the Klan came up often.

Some Klan members supported Coolidge's presidential bid. They posted campaign signs on the roadway. They changed the "Cs" in his slogan "Keep Cool with Coolidge" to large "Ks." From a distance, only "KKK" was visible. When people asked Coolidge how he felt about the Klan, he simply did not reply. Finally, an assistant sent out a notice stating that Coolidge was not a member of the Klan and did not have sympathy for them. Reporters argued that Coolidge himself still had not taken a formal stand against the Klan. His assistant then released another statement. It said that those who truly knew Coolidge knew his position on the Klan.

Coolidge never made his feelings about the Klan public. The power of the Klan began to weaken over the next few years after he won the election. The Klan still exits today, but they must follow the law just like everyone else.

Chapter FOUR

The Roaring Twenties

In 1924, most Americans wanted Coolidge to hold office for a second term.

WHEN IT WAS TIME FOR THE 1924 REPUBLICAN Convention, the delegates chose Coolidge as their candidate. They selected Charles Dawes as the vice presidential candidate. Coolidge didn't actively campaign because he did not believe it was dignified for the president to do so. Instead, others campaigned for him. One popular slogan was "Keep Cool with Coolidge."

During the campaign, Coolidge had to face a life-changing trauma. His 16-year-old son, Calvin Jr., was playing a tough tennis match with his brother on the White House lawn when he developed a blister on his foot. The blister grew painful, and a doctor determined that he had blood poisoning. They took Calvin Jr. to the hospital, but the doctors could not cure him. Calvin Jr. died, and his father

was devastated. "When he went, the power and glory of the presidency went with him," he remarked. Looking back, many people believed Coolidge never really recovered from this loss. He seemed to lose interest in the business of being the president.

On Election Day, the Republican Party's opponents, the Democrats, had little chance of winning with Coolidge running as the Republican candidate. At the Democratic Convention, they had a difficult time selecting a candidate. After arguing and voting many times, the Democrats finally chose John W. Davis. But many people in the party did not vote for Davis. Coolidge and Dawes had solid support and easily won the election.

Coolidge was 52 years old when he was sworn in as president for the second time. In keeping with his values, he did not throw a large, elegant ball or an expensive banquet. He liked to keep things simple and quiet. This was oddly out of step with most Americans during this time in American history, which was called the "Roaring Twenties." Many Americans seemed to be celebrating an endless party. Women had more freedom. They had voted for the first time at the beginning of the

The Coolidge family loved animals. They brought a variety of pets to the White House with them, including six dogs and a raccoon named Rebecca, shown here with Mrs. Coolidge.

decade and were moving into the workforce. Many wore short dresses and the newest bobbed hairstyle. Jazz music became the rage, and at parties, people enjoyed a new dance called "the Charleston."

People felt happy and powerful because of the country's strong **economy.** In most businesses, salaries were steady. Some people were earning more than they had in the past. At the same time, new inventions—such as radios, telephones, washing machines, and automobiles—were now available. People wanted to buy luxuries they once had only dreamed of owning.

During the 1920s, Americans believed that there was nothing that the United States couldn't do better than the rest of the world. Aviation—the science of flying aircraft—took off. Charles Lindbergh became a national hero when he flew his plane, *The Spirit of St. Louis,* solo across the Atlantic Ocean. The great baseball player Babe Ruth hit a new record of 60 home runs. Americans felt great pride in their country.

Coolidge remained calm during this burst of energy in the country. He did little to

During President Coolidge's term of office, Charles Lindbergh became the first pilot to fly solo across the Atlantic Ocean.

change things, and people were happy that he was in the White House. The economy was growing swiftly, and Coolidge encouraged businesses to expand. He helped the economy grow by cutting taxes and paying off some of the national debt, money that the country had borrowed from banks and other sources.

Not everyone was enjoying such success at the time. Farmers were one group that was not doing well during the 1920s. They had too many crops and nowhere to sell them.

Twice Coolidge **vetoed** a bill that would have helped farmers sell crops to other countries. He did this because he thought the government should not interfere in business.

As president, Coolidge worked to keep peace in the world. When **revolutions** broke out in Central America, he sent troops to control them. He sent Ambassador Dwight Morrow to Mexico to stop a war and to protect the right of the United States to mine there. Another Coolidge assistant, Frank Kellogg, even went on to work with French leaders on the Kellogg-Briand Pact of 1928. This **treaty** asked nations to stop using war as a way to solve disagreements. Fifteen nations signed the treaty. Although it did not end war in the long run, the treaty was a step in the right direction.

Near the end of his first full term, Coolidge surprised the country with a short announcement. On August 2, 1927, Coolidge said,

President Coolidge opened the White House weekly to the public. Crowds of people would march through the White House to shake the president's hand. Coolidge once shook 2,096 hands in one hour!

"I do not choose to run for president in 1928." No one was quite sure why he made this decision. He was a popular president who probably would have easily won another term. Whatever the reason, Coolidge stuck to his word.

After Republican Herbert Hoover became the new president in 1929, Coolidge and his family returned to their house in Northampton. They found that they had little privacy there. Reporters and eager citizens bothered them all the time. Finally, the Coolidges bought a 12-room home nearby called "The Beeches." It was surrounded by several acres of land and a gate that gave the family more privacy.

Coolidge kept his law office, but he did not practice law. He served on the board of directors for a large company, which means he helped its leaders make important decisions. He also wrote his autobiography, the story of his life. He authored a regular newspaper column called "Thinking Things Over with Calvin Coolidge." Mr. and Mrs. Coolidge traveled and lived a quiet life.

In June of 1931, Coolidge stopped writing his daily column to spend more time at his family's farm in Plymouth Notch.

He told his family and friends that he often felt tired, even doing normal everyday activities. He said that he felt older than he really was. On January 5, 1933, after a typical morning of checking his mail and working a crossword puzzle, Coolidge went upstairs to shave. Grace Coolidge found the former president on the bathroom floor a short time later. He had died suddenly of a heart attack at the age of 60.

After he retired from the presidency, Coolidge loved to spend time working on his Vermont farm.

Calvin Coolidge died just as he had lived—quietly. He spent the last years of his life in the Vermont farm country where he was born and raised. It was a land he found stirring in its beauty, and it was a land that he loved. After a memorial service that thousands of people attended, Coolidge was buried in his family plot in Plymouth Notch, Vermont.

DURING COOLIDGE'S TIME AS PRESIDENT, A FEW PEOPLE GREW VERY RICH. Most workers did not see a huge growth in their salaries, however. At the same time, advertisers began tempting the public to buy new gadgets that would make their lives better. Everyone longed for the things that rich people had. To help them buy things they wanted, businesses began to offer them a new option called credit. Using credit, people could buy something immediately and then pay for it later. People bought many things that they could not afford and did not save their money as they had in the past.

As the economy grew, the wealthy invested money in the **stock market.** Those with less money also wanted to get rich by investing. Many people had to borrow money to buy stocks. As they invested, the stock market went up. When the stock market went down a little, President Coolidge would assure the people that the economy was still strong. This made the public feel secure, and they invested more money. After a few years, people who had borrowed money for goods or to invest needed to start paying it back. Suddenly, they could no longer buy any new things. Many could not even pay their bills.

What goes up must come down—and that's exactly what happened with the stock market. Just seven months after Coolidge left Washington, the stock market crashed. Many people lost money that day. The photograph at right was taken at the New York Stock Exchange the day after the crash, as people lined up to better understand what had happened. The United States fell into the worst economic time in history, called the Great Depression. Millions of businesspeople lost all their money and had to shut down their companies. Workers couldn't find jobs, and people were left

homeless and without food. In the early 1930s, when the Depression was at its worst, 15 million Americans were out of work.

Looking back, some historians think that Coolidge saw the Depression coming. They believe that was why he did not seek another term as president. They think he did not want to take the blame for the upcoming bad times. In his retirement, Coolidge commented on the Depression: "There has been a general lack of judgment so widespread as to involve practically the whole country. We have learned that we were not so big as we thought we were. We shall have to keep nearer to the ground. We shall not feel so elated, but we shall be much safer."

1872 Calvin Coolidge is born on July 4 in Plymouth Notch, Vermont. His parents are John and Victoria Coolidge.

1884 Victoria Coolidge dies following an accident with a runaway horse.

1890 Abigail Coolidge becomes very ill with appendicitis. Calvin stays by her side until she dies. Coolidge graduates from the Black River Academy in Ludlow, Vermont.

1895 Coolidge graduates from Amherst College with honors. He begins working as an assistant at a law firm in Northampton, Massachusetts.

1897 Calvin Coolidge passes an exam that allows him to practice law in Massachusetts. He opens his first law office. He also begins to work for the Republican Party.

1898 Coolidge is elected city councilman of Northampton, Massachusetts.

1900 Coolidge wins the office of city attorney of Northampton.

1905 On October 4, Coolidge marries Grace Anna Goodhue.

1906 Coolidge is elected to the Massachusetts House of Representatives.

1909 Coolidge is elected mayor of Northampton.

1912 Coolidge becomes a member of the Massachusetts State Senate.

1914 Coolidge serves as president of the Massachusetts State Senate.

1915 Coolidge is elected lieutenant governor of Massachusetts.

1919 Coolidge becomes the governor of Massachusetts, winning the election by almost 17,000 votes. The Boston police force goes on strike, leaving the city without peace-keepers. Coolidge calls in the National Guard to take control of the city. He supports the police commissioner's decision to fire the striking police. President Wilson writes to Coolidge to praise him for his actions.

1920 The Republican Party chooses Warren G. Harding as its presidential candidate. Coolidge is chosen as its vice presidential candidate. Harding and Coolidge win the election.

1923 President Harding takes a long trip across the country to meet with the American people. On August 2, he dies in San Francisco. Early the next morning, Coolidge is sworn in as president of the United States in his father's home in Plymouth Notch, Vermont. The Teapot Dome Scandal surfaces, and the American people learn of illegal activities in Harding's cabinet. Coolidge becomes known as a stronger leader.

1924 Calvin Coolidge Jr. dies from blood poisoning after getting a blister while playing tennis on the White House lawn. On November 4, Calvin Coolidge is elected president. Charles Dawes is elected vice president.

1927 Charles Lindbergh begins his historic flight across the Atlantic Ocean. Baseball great Babe Ruth hits a record 60 home runs in one season. Coolidge surprises the nation by announcing he will not seek another term as president.

1928 The Kellogg-Briand Pact is written and signed by 15 nations. This agreement is designed to help nations find new ways to settle their differences instead of going to war.

1929 Herbert Hoover is inaugurated the nation's 31st president. Coolidge returns to Northampton to lead a peaceful life. He writes his autobiography and a daily newspaper column. In October, the stock market crashes, and the United States falls into the Great Depression. By the early 1930s, 15 million Americans are out of work.

1933 On January 5, Calvin Coolidge dies suddenly from a heart attack. He is buried in Plymouth Notch, Vermont.

bill (BILL)
A bill is an idea for a new law that is presented to a group of lawmakers. Coolidge signed a bill that limited the work week to 40 hours for women and children.

bribe (BRYB)
A bribe is a reward (such as money) that is offered in an attempt to get a person to do something wrong. The Teapot Dome Scandal started when oil companies offered a bribe to a member of President Harding's cabinet.

cabinet (KAB-eh-net)
A cabinet is the group of people who advise a president. President Harding allowed Coolidge to sit in on cabinet meetings.

campaign (kam-PAYN)
A campaign is the process of running for an election, including activities such as giving speeches or attending rallies. Coolidge campaigned for the position of governor of Massachusetts.

candidate (KAN-dih-det)
A candidate is a person running in an election. Coolidge was a candidate for many political offices.

delegates (DEL-eh-gitz)
Delegates are people elected to take part in something. Delegates at the 1920 Republican Convention chose Warren G. Harding as their candidate for president.

economy (ee-KON-uh-mee)
An economy is the way money is earned and spent. The nation had a strong economy while Coolidge was president, meaning that it earned a great deal of money.

militia (meh-LISH-uh)
A militia is a volunteer army, made up of citizens who have trained as soldiers. The mayor of Boston called in the state militia during the 1919 Boston police strike.

nomination (nom-ih-NAY-shun)
If someone receives a nomination, he or she is chosen to run for an office, such as the presidency. Calvin Coolidge received a surprise nomination as the Republican candidate for vice president in 1920.

**notary public
(NOH-tuh-ree PUB-lik)**
A notary public is a person who certifies that documents are legal. As a notary public, John Coolidge was able to swear in Calvin Coolidge as president.

**political parties
(puh-LIT-uh-kul PAR-teez)**
Political parties are groups of people who share similar ideas about how to run a government. The Republican Party is one of the nation's two major political parties.

politics (PAWL-uh-tiks)
Politics refers to the actions and practices of the government. The job of city attorney was one of the first positions in politics that Coolidge held.

revolutions (rev-uh-LOO-shunz)
Revolutions are protests and warfare intended to cause a change in government. When revolutions broke out in Central America, Coolidge sent troops to help.

scandal (SKAN-dl)
A scandal is a shameful action that shocks the public. After President Harding died, the country learned about the Teapot Dome Scandal.

stock market (STAWK MAR-kit)
The stock market is where people buy and sell small pieces of ownership in different companies, called "shares" or "stock." Companies share their profits with people who own their stock.

term (TERM)
A term of office is the length of time politicians can keep their positions by law before another election is held. The president's term is four years.

treaty (TREE-tee)
A treaty is a formal agreement between nations. The Kellogg-Briand Pact was a treaty that asked nations to stop using war as a way to solve disagreements.

veterans (VET-er-enz)
A veteran is someone who has served in the military, especially during a war. Coolidge worked to help veterans of World War I find decent places to live.

veto (VEE-toh)
A veto is the president's power to refuse to sign a bill into law. Coolidge vetoed the McNary-Haaugen Farm bill that might have helped struggling farmers.

Our PRESIDENTS

President	Birthplace	Life Span	Presidency	Political Party	First Lady
George Washington	Virginia	1732–1799	1789–1797	None	Martha Dandridge Custis Washington
John Adams	Massachusetts	1735–1826	1797–1801	Federalist	Abigail Smith Adams
Thomas Jefferson	Virginia	1743–1826	1801–1809	Democratic-Republican	widower
James Madison	Virginia	1751–1836	1809–1817	Democratic Republican	Dolley Payne Todd Madison
James Monroe	Virginia	1758–1831	1817–1825	Democratic Republican	Elizabeth Kortright Monroe
John Quincy Adams	Massachusetts	1767–1848	1825–1829	Democratic-Republican	Louisa Johnson Adams
Andrew Jackson	South Carolina	1767–1845	1829–1837	Democrat	widower
Martin Van Buren	New York	1782–1862	1837–1841	Democrat	widower
William H. Harrison	Virginia	1773–1841	1841	Whig	Anna Symmes Harrison
John Tyler	Virginia	1790–1862	1841–1845	Whig	Letitia Christian Tyler / Julia Gardiner Tyler
James K. Polk	North Carolina	1795–1849	1845–1849	Democrat	Sarah Childress Polk

Our PRESIDENTS

President	Birthplace	Life Span	Presidency	Political Party	First Lady
Zachary Taylor	Virginia	1784–1850	1849–1850	Whig	Margaret Mackall Smith Taylor
Millard Fillmore	New York	1800–1874	1850–1853	Whig	Abigail Powers Fillmore
Franklin Pierce	New Hampshire	1804–1869	1853–1857	Democrat	Jane Means Appleton Pierce
James Buchanan	Pennsylvania	1791–1868	1857–1861	Democrat	never married
Abraham Lincoln	Kentucky	1809–1865	1861–1865	Republican	Mary Todd Lincoln
Andrew Johnson	North Carolina	1808–1875	1865–1869	Democrat	Eliza McCardle Johnson
Ulysses S. Grant	Ohio	1822–1885	1869–1877	Republican	Julia Dent Grant
Rutherford B. Hayes	Ohio	1822–1893	1877–1881	Republican	Lucy Webb Hayes
James A. Garfield	Ohio	1831–1881	1881	Republican	Lucretia Rudolph Garfield
Chester A. Arthur	Vermont	1829–1886	1881–1885	Republican	widower
Grover Cleveland	New Jersey	1837–1908	1885–1889	Democrat	Frances Folsom Cleveland

	President	Birthplace	Life Span	Presidency	Political Party	First Lady
	Benjamin Harrison	Ohio	1833–1901	1889–1893	Republican	Caroline Scott Harrison
	Grover Cleveland	New Jersey	1837–1908	1893–1897	Democrat	Frances Folsom Cleveland
	William McKinley	Ohio	1843–1901	1897–1901	Republican	Ida Saxton McKinley
	Theodore Roosevelt	New York	1858–1919	1901–1909	Republican	Edith Kermit Carow Roosevelt
	William H. Taft	Ohio	1857–1930	1909–1913	Republican	Helen Herron Taft
	Woodrow Wilson	Virginia	1856–1924	1913–1921	Democrat	Ellen L. Axson Wilson / Edith Bolling Galt Wilson
	Warren G. Harding	Ohio	1865–1923	1921–1923	Republican	Florence Kling De Wolfe Harding
	Calvin Coolidge	Vermont	1872–1933	1923–1929	Republican	Grace Goodhue Coolidge
	Herbert C. Hoover	Iowa	1874–1964	1929–1933	Republican	Lou Henry Hoover
	Franklin D. Roosevelt	New York	1882–1945	1933–1945	Democrat	Anna Eleanor Roosevelt Roosevelt
	Harry S. Truman	Missouri	1884–1972	1945–1953	Democrat	Elizabeth Wallace Truman

44

Our PRESIDENTS

President	Birthplace	Life Span	Presidency	Political Party	First Lady
Dwight D. Eisenhower	Texas	1890–1969	1953–1961	Republican	Mary "Mamie" Doud Eisenhower
John F. Kennedy	Massachusetts	1917–1963	1961–1963	Democrat	Jacqueline Bouvier Kennedy
Lyndon B. Johnson	Texas	1908–1973	1963–1969	Democrat	Claudia Alta Taylor Johnson
Richard M. Nixon	California	1913–1994	1969–1974	Republican	Thelma Catherine Ryan Nixon
Gerald Ford	Nebraska	1913–	1974–1977	Republican	Elizabeth "Betty" Bloomer Warren Ford
James Carter	Georgia	1924–	1977–1981	Democrat	Rosalynn Smith Carter
Ronald Reagan	Illinois	1911–	1981–1989	Republican	Nancy Davis Reagan
George Bush	Massachusetts	1924–	1989–1993	Republican	Barbara Pierce Bush
William Clinton	Arkansas	1946–	1993–2001	Democrat	Hillary Rodham Clinton
George W. Bush	Connecticut	1946–	2001–	Republican	Laura Welch Bush

Presidential FACTS

Qualifications

To run for president, a candidate must
- be at least 35 years old
- be a citizen who was born in the United States
- have lived in the United States for 14 years

Term of Office

A president's term of office is four years. No president can stay in office for more than two terms.

Election Date

The presidential election takes place every four years on the first Tuesday of November.

Inauguration Date

Presidents are inaugurated on January 20.

Oath of Office

I do solemnly swear I will faithfully execute the office of the President of the United States and will to the best of my ability preserve, protect, and defend the Constitution of the United States.

Write a Letter to the President

One of the best things about being a U.S. citizen is that Americans get to participate in their government. They can speak out if they feel government leaders aren't doing their jobs. They can also praise leaders who are going the extra mile. Do you have something you'd like the president to do? Should the president worry more about the environment and encourage people to recycle? Should the government spend more money on our schools? You can write a letter to the president to say how you feel!

1600 Pennsylvania Avenue
Washington, D.C. 20500

You can even send an e-mail to: president@whitehouse.gov

For Further INFORMATION

Internet Sites

Learn more about the Boston Police Strike of 1919:
http://www.columbia.edu/~zms2/unpublished/thesis/chap1.html

Learn more about Coolidge's character and personality:
http://www.noho.com/calvinc.html

Learn more about Coolidge's cabinet and term in office:
http://www.ipl.org/ref/POTUS/ccoolidge.html

Listen to Coolidge and other leaders of the era give speeches:
http://lcweb2.loc.gov/ammem/nfhome.html

Learn more about the Calvin Coolidge Memorial Foundation:
http://www.calvin-coolidge.org/found.htm

Take a virtual tour of the Calvin Coolidge State Historical Site:
http://www.vtliving.com/historicsites/coolidge

Learn more about all the presidents and visit the White House:
http://www.whitehouse.gov/WH/glimpse/presidents/html/presidents.html
http://www.thepresidency.org/presinfo.htm
http://www.americanpresidents.org/

Books

Hakin, Joy. *War, Peace, and All That Jazz/Book 9* (A History of Us). New York: Oxford University Press, 1995.

Feinberg, Barbara Silberdick. *Black Tuesday: The Stock Market Crash of 1929.* Brookfield, CT: Millbrook Press, 1995.

Kent, Zachary. *Encyclopedia of Presidents.* Chicago: Childrens Press, 1988.

Sandler, Martin W. *Library of Congress Presidents.* New York: Harper Collins, 1995.

Stein, Conrad R. *The Great Depression.* Chicago: Childrens Press, 1994.

Index

jB
COOLIDGE   Maupin, Melissa.

                Calvin Coolidge.

$27.07

DATE